TATUM MOORER

Peace Corps Madagascar

What You Need to Know Before You Go and When You're There

local language and being taught grassroot level work that our respective sectors focused on. We had just started to become accustomed to the insanely hot temperatures when Al-Qaeda invaded northern Niger and we had to be consolidated until it was determined how best to proceed.

After a week of living in limbo, our country director determined that it was not safe or ideal for my cohort to stay and serve in Niger. As a group we were devastated. The Great Recession caused by the housing collapse was still in full swing back in the States and none of us would have jobs if sent back. Luckily, the country of Madagascar was just starting its Peace Corps program back up after being suspended in 2006 for a political coup and would be able to welcome our entire cohort as a whole to help restart the program. (It wasn't until later in our service that we learned this was not typical, instead trainees are usually divided up and either sent to another country that has positions for their sector or are sent back to the States to wait for another invitation at a later date.)

While collectively we were very fortunate to be able to stay together and start our training almost immediately in our new host country, we were very much not prepared for the culture or the environmental change of Madagascar! In this book I go through what new trainees / volunteers should know or expect before getting to site as well as things I wish I would have known before arriving in Madagascar. What follows is my own personal view based on what I experienced during my service. I am not a recruiter and what follows is in no way a direct reflection of the views of the Peace Corps in general.

Note: Sectors define the focus of the overarching job specific details for the position each volunteer is selected to do. The sector types have changed since my time of service and now include Agriculture, Community Economic Development, Education, Environment, Health, and Youth in Development.

A Brief Overview of Madagascar

Madagascar is the fourth largest island in the world, roughly the size of Texas and the length of the western United States coast. The island's climate is tropical along the coast, temperate inland, and arid in the south. The island is home to mountainous plateaus, dry deserts, rich rainforests as well as tropical dry forests. The south has an arid climate, whereas the interior has a temperate temperature. Some of the greatest coral reef systems and most extensive mangrove habitats in the Western Indian Ocean are found along its more than 3,000 miles of coastline. The hot, wet season extends from November to April and the cooler, drier season from May to October.

Since separating from the African continent an estimated 160 million years ago, the island nation of Madagascar has formed its own unique ecosystems and amazing species. The island is home to a wide variety of vegetation and animals. About 92% of Madagascar's mammals, 9% of its plants, and 95% of its reptiles have never been seen before on Earth. There are more than 11,000 indigenous plant species, including seven different varieties of baobab trees, as well as a wide range of mammals, reptiles, amphibians, and insects. Madagascar has several critically endangered species and unique habitats threatened by demands from today's global markets and from the growing needs of the local population.

Though located about 250 miles off the Southeastern coast of the African

1

Less Is More

Personally, I think the least amount of research you do before going to your host country the better off you'll be. Now, I know I said in the intro above that I wasn't prepared for the culture and environmental change - which is true! - but unexpectedly going from the hottest country inhabited by humans to what then felt like a chilly rainforest, one can never be prepared. What I mean by doing minimal research is only reading the brief synopsis of information Peace Corps provides you with in your invitation, and maybe finding a blog or two written by current volunteers, then calling it good. By doing this I found that it was easier to be more open to learning about exactly where I was and who I was with, rather than going in with assumptions of how it was going to be.

You will receive a lot of information about the different tribes and cultures during your pre-service training, much of which you can't learn about from research as things are ever changing. Plus, Madagascar is so much larger than people realize it is, and the customs, environment, taboos, and norms are all so different from region to region that anything you research beforehand may not even apply to where you end up on the

Isolation & Time Alone

Another thing Volunteers and **Peace Corps** staff will tell you is that being alone and isolated at site is **extremely hard**; this is real, it is SO hard! Even if you are an outgoing and friendly person there will be times that you will feel utterly alone and **at a loss**. During the first two weeks at site everyone feels like a fish out of water, but still slightly optimistic that things are going well. It's right after week two where most everyone typically crashes and has a small sort of isolation breakdown; it is hard to describe unless one has gone through it, which unfortunately I feel like now I have an example! The best thing I can compare the isolated feeling to is the very beginning of Covid-19. Just like in the beginning, when everyone was staying home or distancing themselves, and struggling to cope with how society was changing and how to survive, that is exactly what it is going to feel like from time to time during your service. Being alone is part of the Peace Corps **package**, it allows you to really reflect and discover who you are as your **own person**, but it isn't always fun or easy.

Everyone handles these hard times differently, some get through it by leaving their house and trying to integrate into their village, others reach out to fellow cohorts and Peace Corps neighbors to have conversations, some volunteers journal, while others will read a book. In the end getting through the tough alone times comes down a lot to how fast you can process your feelings and adjust your outlook on what it is that created the spiral, which can be extremely hard. Then throw in a little homesickness in there and you'll wonder how anyone completes their two years of service. Overall, this feeling sucks and there is no way to really avoid it, you just have to mentally know that it is going to happen and figure out what will work best for you to get through it.

All Eyes on You: How You'll Have Close to Zero Privacy

Now just because one is technically isolated from the people they know and the familiar norms they're used to does not, by any means, mean that they are alone. Depending on the size of the village or town you live in you may very well may be the source of entertainment for the entire village. All eyes will be on you all the time. Which can either be good and bad, all depending on your mood at that moment. It is great when you don't want to be alone but also borderline annoying when you want to work on something that requires focus and being alone which may prove to be rather challenging.

After a while I learned that in most rural villages it's uncommon for people to have alone time or to be by themselves. Many Malagasy families live in one room houses with three generations under one roof, so it is uncommon for them to have any alone time at all, thus they don't understand how you can be okay being on your own. Most often neighboring kids were at my house a lot, mostly because I was different and that was exciting to them. It may also be due to the fact that I was willing to be silly and actually spend time with them, as Malagasy adults don't always have time to play with their kids as there are other things they must do.

Another thing I had to get used to was kids and adults coming by saying they heard I bought tomatoes (or did something) that day when in fact this was the first time I was seeing them that day; it was because I really was their entertainment! Everyone knows everyone so people will in fact talk about you and you just have to accept and be okay with it. It took me longer to adjust to being someone that is always having attention as I was, and still am, a very introverted person. For me, at times it made me feel like I was part of the community, as people were really looking out for my well-being. Other times I would wish that I could just buy tomatoes like a normal anonymous person and not like a local make-shift celebrity.

3

Interview for Site Placement

Before being assigned a site you'll go through a bit of an interview process at the beginning of your training in Montasoa. It's during these conversations and interviews that you want to really be transparent about what you want to get out of your service and what you're wanting in a site. I should also note that interviews conducted at Pre-Service Training was how site assignments were done around 2010, the process very well could be different now. Here's some particular bullets that I would it be wise to bring up:

Speak Up if you're LGBTQIA+

If you are a member of the LGBTQIA+ community, and you plan to be open about your status during your service, I would recommend letting your supervisors know as there are some regions in Madagascar that are way more reserved in thinking than others. The Peace Corps wants all volunteers to stay and thrive in their village, not end your service early because you feel unsafe or are targeted negatively.

One of my cohorts who was gay visited me at my site and my community didn't understand why one would " want" to be gay... it was an interesting conversation but luckily that was all it was. The first five minutes every single person said it was not okay to be gay and appeared to be very stern about their conviction. Then around minute 6 people either recalled someone they knew who was gay, or talk about somebody in the neighboring town who was trans, and others would respond with happiness and non-bias on how much they liked that person. This was just my experience at my site! This may not be how a conversation may go in another region. I would highly recommend talking to someone who works at Peace Corps Madagascar, Volunteers who are currently serving in-country, and any of the Malagasy staff you feel comfortable with on the typical views or standings of the regions if you have any concerns.

For more information about serving as an LGBTQIA+ volunteer please go to: https://www.peacecorps.gov/stories/9-questions-about-serving-as-an-lgbtqia-volunteer-answered/ for some common questions and answers, and I would recommend seeking out blog posts and reading a previous volunteer's account of their experience at: https://www.peacecorps.gov/stories/living-the-questions-hiding-identity-as-a-an-lgbtqia-volunteer/

Structure vs Less Structure (NGO or counterpart)

If you are someone who would rather work with a bit more structure you'll want to tell your interviewer as there will be a few site assignments that will partner with an NGO. The NGO will act more as an anchor point and guide for your work, sometimes you'll be working with them a lot while other times you may be doing a smaller project on your own. If you are someone who would prefer to go with the flow and figure things out as you go, you should tell your interviewer that as well. Most likely you'll be partnered with an individual from the community as a point of contact, and you may choose to work or not work with this person during your service. I was fortunate that I had a counterpart who was very motivated and supportive while I was in-country, however there were other volunteers who didn't get along with the counterpart initially assigned to them and they found someone else in their community to collaborate with.

Size of Village/City

You will also want to tell them the size of the village or town you would prefer to live in. There are trade-offs for every size of sites and these can really either help one as a volunteer wither or thrive. For me I asked for a small to medium-sized village because I wanted to have a sense of community, and really know my neighbors, while potentially having some anonymity. There were volunteers who wanted to live in larger towns or a city setting, as they always wanted to have some comforts of home and be more anonymous; but with that came the trade-off of being slightly more isolated and being treated like a tourist rather than a member of the community. Other volunteers wanted to really rough it and be as far away from city life as possible, so they would usually be stationed in a smaller village but the trade-off would usually be a long and unpleasant ride to and from their banking town each month. If you are honest with yourself, you'll know what type of environment you'll thrive better in.

Weather

As silly as this may sound, Madagascar has almost every kind of environment and weather you can imagine on the island, with the exception of tundra and snow. If you know the type of weather you have to live in in order to perform your best you should let your interviewer know. For some that included some rainy afternoons and some humidity, for others that meant having hills or mountains nearby, and others wanted dry flat plains. For me I needed sunshine and drier heat, I didn't want to be cold, so that is what I told them in my interview. Luckily for me they had a site that fit my request perfectly!

Things to Remember

Don't expect your site to tick every single box on your want list. Most sites don't have electricity or running water, most won't have good roads or the weather you like with the type of work environment you want to be in. This is not a luxury experience so don't be surprised if you only get one thing on the list that you want. If you are open and flexible with your placement, and only give your interviewer one or two things that are important to you to have with a site, they'll assign you to a place where you can potentially flourish.

4

Things to Expect When at Site

Installation: Getting Dropped Off

Before going into the Peace Corps I read in a book about a volunteer who chased after the car that dropped her off in her village that first day and I thought, "How ridiculous is that!?" But then I got to my site and I understood completely what that volunteer must have felt as that was exactly how I felt, terrified! By the end of training, everyone is full of anticipation to get to site and start their Peace Corps journey, but it is terrifying when you realize you are going to be all alone in a very foreign place, with nothing familiar around and only being able to rely on yourself to get through it. It can be hard to stand there and wave as Peace Corps drives away and you have to try to figure out what you should do next. There is the possibility that you may be so distracted with people coming out and wanting to welcome you (or you're informed that you'll be making a speech in front of the whole village in an hour-and-a-half at your welcome ceremony) that you'll be too busy to notice as the car drives away. In any case, installation day is one of the biggest and most memorable days of one's volunteer service and it is totally normal to be terrified when the car pulls away.

Stay in Your Village but Get out of Your House

After arriving (and being left) at site one of your first instincts will either be to flee from your site or isolate yourself inside your house; do your best to fight these feelings! It is extremely hard to stay somewhere where you don't know anyone, struggle with understanding and communicating with others, all while having no idea what you should be doing. However, you need to do it in order to become better acquainted and integrated within your community. I would suggest starting with small goals, like getting out of your house and going for a short walk. Or going to the market and buying two things, you might have a list of 13 items but if you only buy five you should celebrate as those are small victories! Most likely on these walks you'll be joined by children or teens and you'll get to know a bit more of the layout and things to do at your site. It is hard at first but pushing yourself to leave your house will make you feel like you accomplished something everyday.

The People

Malagasy people are very friendly people, they're also very direct or blunt as well. They will be the first to tell you that you don't know how to speak malagasy very well, as if you didn't know, or that the food you made tastes bad. And sometimes they will just say things that we as Americans are not used to hearing said to our face. At first it can be hard to take feedback in such a way, your feelings may be hurt but that is usually not their intention, Malagasy are simply trying to tell you something that they may believe you may not know. My Village had a lot of ladies and teenagers with very wicked senses of humor, and that caused a whole mess of fun for the community members when I first arrived, and quite a bit of confusion for me. But it led to us having great inside jokes and a sense of comradery while also giving me permission to be silly and letting me know it was okay to mess up.

Later on in my service I discovered that a lot of the time when Malagasy were telling me I wasn't good at something was their way of telling me that they wanted to show me how they did whatever task that it was. For example, almost every volunteer has been told at one time or another they don't know how to cook and it's not so much that we don't know how to cook, it's just that we cook in a different way (and with way less salt in the beginning). That then leaves the opportunity to ask if someone can help teach you how to cook like a Malagasy, to which they'll be more than happy to send their eight-year-old over to teach you how to prepare food like a local. So while direct feedback may sound like criticism at first, learning how to turn it into an opportunity to better understand something that will make creating friendships easier.

Work & Projects at Site

One of the things that took me by surprise when I first got to site was how much stress I had over not being stressed over work like I was in the States. It is jarring to not have work to attend to at first, as most of us in the States are programed with the work mentality, and though focusing on the second goal of Peace Corps (sharing American Culture with the host country) is what you're encouraged to focus on the first year of service it is still hard to not have any idea what you should be doing. I found out that I was not the only new volunteer that had these feelings at first, but after a few months, we all got used to the slower pace of each day and were able to learn more about what may be needed in our communities.

Goals and project plans don't always work out. During pre-service training you're going to have so many ideas of projects that you'll want to do and most of the time that are not what you whined up doing. While it is good to go with some thoughts of projects that you may like to do, because ultimately there will be a time in your service where you can do that mural that you thought of or can conduct a class on compost, but you won't truly know what your community needs or wants until you get to site. I only achieved two of the initial things that I had on my project list during my three years, the rest had already been done or didn't apply to the environment at my site. While at first I was disappointed that I couldn't do what I initially planned to do, I found that by being open and flexible to the type of projects the community was needing or wanting actually made for a more unique experience and was more satisfying than the projects I had wanted to do in the first place.

Peace Corps projects will depend on your site, the type of environment it's located in, along with how motivated the people are in your community. For me and my site, I had an extremely motivated community so we got a lot done during my time of service, but some of the other volunteers only got one or two projects done that they wanted to achieve, and really that was okay! Everyone will have a completely different experience with their site projects and most of them will be totally different and unique to your village, so there is no need to compare your project to another.

In Terms of Housing...

Every site must provide their volunteers with housing and their own latrine, however, the condition and square footage of these dwellings have no requirement, so no place is exactly like another. Some of the sites will have electricity, some have running water, some are made out of wood, others out of stone; some dwellings are stand-alone, while others are apartments, some will have yards while others may only have a stoop. Overall it really will depend on the region you're in and what sector you're in that may influence the type of housing sites have to offer.

Many volunteer homes would have dwellings with either one very large room, that would house their kitchen, bed and their work area, or they'd have two rooms. Showers were located either as an attached room or away from the house, and most didn't have running water so bucket baths were the norm. Which honestly was rather nice in the winter as we learned how to wash/bathe with our clothes on and it also made us appreciate when we were able to have access to a real shower. As for latrines and the condition of which they are in, it is entirely dependent on the host village and what they have to provide. In the rural areas the likelihood of it being a wooden out-house were high, in larger cities having a porcelain squat toilet wasn't unheard of, and in other places there might be a sit-down toilet like we're used to in the States. However, the infrastructure in Madagascar does not allow for the flushing of toilet paper, instead there's a wastebasket typically located next to the toilet for you to discard your used paper in there. It was a little weird at first but we got used to it quickly.

My house was a total of 120 square feet, including a 40 square foot porch, and was made of wood. There were gaps between the planks, the wind was able to blow through the walls (which during the summer was always wonderful but during the winter was absolutely miserable) but there was no way to really stop it so I just had to get used to it. I had a room I used as my kitchen and socializing room, a 4'x4' platform for my shower attached to my main room, and a latrine made of stone that I shared with my neighbors that was about 20 yards away from my house. I was not able to have a full size bed, instead I had a twin bed and that allowed me to have more space rather than just a room with a bed in it. I was one of the few volunteers to have access to electricity; I had one plug-in for charging my phone and one light for each room (however I was only able to have one light on at a time at night otherwise it would short-circuit the generator and me and my neighbor would lose power).

5

Everyone's Favorite Thing... Food!

While everyone thinks that living on a tropical island means that one will be able to enjoy a delicious balanced diet I must warn you this is a false notion. Just because you're in Madagascar, where many types of fruits and foods are able to grow, that does not mean that you will have access to them nor does it mean everything is available year round. You will learn about there being seasons for food; it is not like the States where you can have any type of fruit or vegetable year-round. In fact, there are many places in Madagascar where you won't even have access to half of the items you wanted. In some areas you'll be eating rice and green leaves for most of the year, while in other areas you'll debate between the type of beans you'll eat that day. The menu can be very monotonous and boring, but after a while that can become comforting because then it's one less decision that you have to make that day. And by the time your second year rolls around you have a better understanding and appreciation for the seasons and actually have something to look forward to - like mango season in December and tomato season in the summer!

Again, the size of your site and where it is located on the island will influence the type of food that is available to you on a daily basis. If you live in a larger town there are more food options to choose from at the market, however, food is usually more expensive in these locations. There's always the option of going out for dinner, as you will learn where the cheapest restaurants are and prepared street food may be available for cheaper than the ingredients to make something yourself; but again this is only really an option if you live in a medium sized village to larger town.

If you live in a smaller village you may find that street food and places to eat out are slim to none. You most likely won't have as much food selection at site but the price for what is grown locally will be much cheaper than what is in town. If you choose to cook for yourself you'll come to find that cooking will take up a good chunk of your day; it will take a while before you figure out how to whittle cooking time down. If you are not much of a cook other arrangements can be made such as preparing and eating dinner with a Malagasy family that you feel close with. With this approach it is best to talk with the lady of the household and either arrange a money stipend you should contribute for food or discuss what actual food you can purchase for the meals. A number of my cohorts ate dinner with their neighbors or counterpart's families as it gave them time to visit, learn more about the culture and lessened the burden of making food for one.

For most volunteers who live in rural villages, going into town and buying a meal at a restaurant or from a street vendor is usually a special treat - even if the food selections at sit down places weren't typically varied much from what they're eating back at site. After a while every volunteer will have their personal favorite places to frequent or items to eat each time they come into town. For some volunteers they would treat themselves to a steak-frete dinner, while others would seek out chicken in tomato sauce. Each volunteer had their own thing and if you were only able to have it once a month made it that much better. For me, I loved treating myself to bananas and cold yogurt for breakfast when I went to my banking town. (Having access to ripe bananas really ruined any bananas back in the states, they just don't taste as good as the ones there.) I would also treat myself to the dessert of fried bananas in the evening and with my banking town being near the ocean I was also able to get oysters rather cheap anytime they were available in town.

Things to Expect Outside of Your Site

Leaving Your Site

When I was a volunteer we were paid every month, so we would have three days to go to our banking town and pick up our money to last us for the month. If one lived close to their baking town it was a nice three day break, but if one lived farther away it meant that they really only had one day to enjoy the city before having to turn around and go back to site. Peace Corps Madagascar has had much debate over how many days volunteers should have for banking; some think that only one day is needed while others think we should have a week. For many volunteers living in rural areas, traveling to our banking town is really the only time that we get a mental break from our site. It is the only time during the month where we're able to be slightly anonymous and don't necessarily have to fit in. (Granted we were seen and treated as foreigners/ tourists so that provides its own set of issues but after a while it's a price most of us are happy to pay.)

During our banking days we are also more likely to have access to more reliable internet and a wider variety of food. Usually mail can be delivered in this town and if you were to receive packages you will be paying for them as the cost of freight in the country is not covered by the cost of freight from the States. Many banking towns may have Peace Corps Volunteers living there, as in it is their site, so if you're lucky and on good terms with them they may be willing to allow you to stay at their place for free. There is an etiquette when wanting to stay with a Volunteer in town and that is you need to call and ask them first as sometimes they are out of town or they really just don't want people around; don't take it personally if they say no.

Besides a mental health break from site, banking also allows for you to get uninterrupted work done, meet up with other volunteers in your region and sometimes go on a day trip somewhere nearby. Most likely by the end of your service you'll be better friends with your neighboring Peace Corps Volunteers than those that you went through training with, as you will see them and have similar experiences/regional problems than your cohorts in other parts of the island. That isn't to say that you'll do your vacations or traveling with your neighbors, that is still usually done with those cohorts that you don't see as often and a lot of that has to do with timing and training.

Vacations & Traveling

During your service there are many opportunities for you to take advantage of traveling and exploring is highly encouraged! The Peace Corps has a rule that you are not allowed to travel outside of your site/banking region until after your first in service training (which typically takes place between the third and sixth month after installation) and most Volunteers don't have enough money or vacation time saved up for trips until then anyway. However, even after that time, you will still have to ask for permission to leave or be away from your site to go on vacation. You should submit your itinerary at least a month ahead of your planned trip as your supervisor will need to receive your request, sign off on it, and send it back to you before you're allowed to go anywhere. If you're caught out of site without permission, the Peace Corps does have grounds for ending your service and sending you back to the States. (Note: this didn't happen to anyone while I was in Madagascar, however probations and severe warnings were issued to some).

Most volunteers plan vacations around their in-service trainings, as they take place in a more central location of the island and make it easier to get to the destinations they want to go. Also for volunteers that live in fly sites, their airfare is paid for by the Peace Corps to get to the training and thus it is cheaper for them to get out of their region for travel at that time. If you do not live at a fly-site but want to go somewhere that requires a flight, you yourself will have to fund your airplane ticket, as the Peace Corps will not pay for it. Most travel will occur via taxi brouse and will be with local Malagasy people, who will wonder what you are doing traveling in a taxi brouse instead of the typical private car other foreigners travel in. Many of the roads you'll be traveling on are either extremely windy or are in terrible condition, and sometimes they're both! I never got motion sickness before Peace Corps, however I became a regular subscriber to Dramamine in order to survive the long taxi brouse travel days in my region without getting sick.

Traveling in a private car can be much more tolerable but they are more expensive and most volunteers would rather splurge on good food and a nice place to stay rather than private transportation when going on a trip. That doesn't mean there aren't some random and good deals out there or the once-in-a-lifetime modes that can be utilized. For example one of my PCV neighbors was traveling up the South East Coast and the road was washed out; she just happened to meet some gendarme pilots flying up to the location she wanted to go so she bargained for a ride for a ride in their helicopter. While that fight was a little pricey on a Peace

Corps salary it was well worth her money as it saved her time and misery of finding another way to her destination.

Identification

Whether you're traveling on vacation or to your neighboring town you should always carry your blue card and your Xerox copy of your passport. Typically there are checkpoints in and out of each town by the gendarme and if they see you they will ask for your papers or identification, if you do not have your ID they may detain you there at the outskirts of town while your transportation goes on its way. They could also demand a bribe from you and, since you're a foreigner, it will not be a small one like the locals would pay. This happened to me on my first trip out of my village to the neighboring town and the only reason the gendarme did not detain me was because the local people I was traveling with in the brouse informed him that I lived in my village with them. It took a long time to convince him of this, and I think my driver did pay a small bribe to get me through the checkpoint, but eventually they let me go. After a while, if you're in a rural area, the gendarme in your region will eventually come to know you and won't check your identification upon entry or exit of the town, but if you are traveling to other less familiar towns then you will for sure want to have your ID.

Prices

When traveling outside of your site you should expect to pay more for almost everything because you will be seen as a foreigner. Yes, in your regional and local people will come to know you and eventually you'll learn how to haggle to get the real price of things – and eventually they'll give it to you without you needing to haggle – but when you travel to other parts of the island that will almost never be the case. Food at restaurants will be priced as listed so there is no upcharge or haggling that will need to take place, however, vendors and marketplace areas you will have to barter the price down. As hotels and some adventures are typical for tourists to partake in, you will most likely be paying the full price for these experiences. There are some volunteers who can actually haggle and finagle a good price on everything, including tourist trips, so if you have one of these people as your friend/in your travel group they will really help you all save money. However, it's better to be prepared to pay full price for everything and try to focus more on having a good time when you can and save your money in some areas.

Taboo Culture

Should you be visiting other Volunteers at their sites while on vacation (or just for fun) it is important to ask what they do and don't do at their site. For example, a lot of volunteers won't drink at their site simply because they don't want to have the reputation of being drunk or opening themselves up to something that could be misinterpreted. They are also better knowledgeable in their Villages or region's taboos and things that you should avoid or not do as the locals will either become offended or look down on you for it. Taboos truly vary in subject and reason from village to village and region to region, but they should be taken seriously so as not to make yourself or your fellow PCVs an outcast or target.

In my region it was taboo to eat turtle or have anything to do with a snake (besides killing it), in some regions it was taboo to eat pig and after watching what pigs eat and what's under some of their skin a lot of other Malagasy will avoid eating pig as well. Then there are some taboos that will make no sense in our minds such as having twins; yes, there is a region of the island where having twins was considered to be taboo and the people would give them to orphanages in other areas where this taboo didn't apply. It was very funny when one Peace Corps Volunteer, who was a triplett, was stationed in this region as his two brothers came from the states to visit him at one point during his service and this made for some interesting introductions at his site.

Souvenirs

When coming back to your site from any overnight trip, people in your community will most likely expect you to bring back gifts or souvenirs for them. (Yes, this includes every time you go to your banking town.) Again the Malagasy people are very direct and straightforward about their expectations of a gift, however you should not feel obligated to bring souvenirs back every time. It takes a while to learn who you will bring things back to and who you don't bother with. I found that any time I brought any sort of material possession for anyone that they didn't really find it as valuable or like it as much as I thought they would, or they would be complain that the shirt was red and not blue or their friend would ask to have it and they'd to give it to them because they didn't buy it. In the end I wound up bringing only my friend and counterpart's wife gifts of fresh food or scarce items that we didn't have in my region, such as green beans or spices; that way they was able to have a treat of sorts, as well as able to ration and share it with everyone in the family. Some people will always ask for a souvenir and complain when you don't give them any, but really you shouldn't feel bad about not bringing anyone back anything. Just share and bring gifts to those who you really care about and they will usually be happy and find value in what you bring to them.

II

What I Wish I Knew

7

What I Should Have Packed

Hindsight is always 20/20. While I wasn't originally slated to serve in Madagascar that doesn't mean there weren't a number of things I really wish I knew before going into the Peace Corps - as well as while I was there.First and foremost I wish I would have known what to and not to pack. Peace Corps usually will send a list of suggested items to bring with after you accept your invitation, but a lot of the time it's more of a guideline and not a for sure bring this list type of list. Here is the list of things I wish I would have seriously known to bring with me:

Electronics

I really wish I would have taken a laptop with me. Not a fancy laptop but a laptop that could have been dinged up and banged around a lot while still operating. I would also advise it being a laptop that one is not totally attached to, so if someone should happen to take it off of you it would not be the end of your world. As long as it has Microsoft Office, the ability to connect to the internet, and possibly a media viewer on it that is seriously all that you need on there. Bring a portable harddrive (or two) to store movies, photos and music on and keep them in a separate bag/place than your laptop and life will be much better.

I'd also encourage any electronics that allow you to listen to music or downloaded podcasts as taxi brouse rides can be really long and sometimes it's nice to just have the time to listen to something. When I started my service smartphones were not the norm, the Apple Store was the only place that distributed them, so we all had either an iPod or MP3 player.

I am not sure what the phone service is currently like in Madagascar so they may or may not work like they do in the States. However, the good thing with the smartphone is that it comes with a built in camera that you can use to take pictures and videos on. This has allowed volunteers to update their experiences with people back home and share project progress with those who help fund site projects. Should you choose to bring your own phone I'd recommend making sure that it is unlocked, can have two SIM cards, and that it not be the top-of-the-line new phone as the likelihood of it breaking or being stolen is rather high. If you don't want to bring your own you can purchase a phone that will most likely be cheaper and easier to use while in-country. Again it has been almost ten years since I've been on the island so they might have more cellular towers, internet and technology that actually works, however I would definitely not rely or expect that to be the case. There were plenty of volunteers that I knew that would literally have to hike a mountain in order to get any sort of phone reception so you may not be able to be in constant contact with others all the time. (Obviously bring adapters as well as backup cords for your laptop and any other electronics you have.)

Clothing

I also really wish that I took good quality rain gear. A lightweight, thin rain jacket that can wick away water quickly and efficiently but keep me dry would have been a plus. Yes, you can buy clothes there, however, the good quality items will most likely be outside of your Peace Corps budget, possibly not available in your region, and the cheaper versions won't always work as well. If you're in the rainforest or stationed in an area that's prone to rain all the time, good rain gear is something that you're going to want to be of good quality.

I also wish I took warmer clothes in general. Being from a state that's known for being cold during the winter I figured I didn't really need to worry about winter clothing going to the hottest inhabitable place on earth or a tropical island. I learned the hard way that after a year of living somewhere you adapt to the warm weather and it no longer feels hot, and that means that what locals consider to be cold weather actually feels very cold even though the temperature is between 60 day 90 degrees! You may look at the packing suggestion list and be like, "Why would I take Birkenstocks? This is ridiculous!" and then year two you'll be like, "Thank gawd I brought these Birkenstocks!" I seriously wish I took warmer clothes.

I'd pretty much recommend bringing any items of quality such as a few pair of socks, one good pair of shoes, some sandals, one or two pairs of jeans, a good coat, and some work gloves. Again, you can buy plenty of t-shirts, pants and clothing items from second hand sellers but items that are of quality are sometimes really hard to come by and it's worth bringing those with you rather than trying to find them on the island.

Gear

Camping gear is also another thing that I wish I took with me. Again, the thought of needing a sleeping bag was laughable but it would have been great to have for traveling and cooler nights. A small tent would have come in handy as it allowed for the volunteers that brought them to have a lot more options when traveling as they didn't have to rent anything. Also a blow up sleeping pad would have been nice as there wasn't always bed space when crashing with other volunteers. Honestly, those who had a blow up pad, almost everybody wound up using theirs during the last few months at sight due to the flatness of their mattresses so I would highly recommend bringing one.

I would also say I should have brought more duct tape with me as well as multiple headlamps as one always breaks or gets lost and having a good reliable backup is nice. Not that you can't find a replacement one in a marketplace, but it'll most likely be more expensive and of cheaper quality. Duct tape should be self-explanatory, you'd be surprised what all you can use it with.

If you're not going to bring a sleeping bag I would then recommend either buying or bringing some bedding that you don't mind leaving behind at the end of your service. Sleeping is not always an easy thing to come by during your service but one of the happiest places will be your bed and it's really nice to have one that is comfortable to be in. (Which leads me to jump ahead a little but when you are buying supplies for your site before installation I would highly recommend buying a high quality mattress! Most mattresses in Madagascar are made of foam, and they work alright in the beginning but after two years they turn into something similar to a yoga mat and they don't do much in terms of support. If you can find and are willing to splurge on a good mattress I highly recommend doing so as it will make your life so much better!)

Spices

I would bring a shit ton of spices! While Madagascar has the ability to grow so much food, and such a wide variety of it, that doesn't mean there will be a lot of food or variety where you live. This is true for spices too.

Everywhere on the island you will find the main ingredients Malagasy use to flavor their food are salt, pepper and curry powder along with onions, garlic and ginger. There is also a hot chile pepper and vinegar topping that will coat the inside of your mouth with such a burning sensation that you won't taste anything that goes in your mouth for 20 minutes after you eat it but that is typically that is it for flavoring food. Some areas in the North have saffron or turmeric or a couple other options but overall spices and herbs are very limited, so if you want to have various flavors with your food I'd recommend bringing a lot of your favorite spices with you.

8

Wildlife

Another thing that I wish I would have known about was the wildlife that I would frequently see. Yes, there are lemurs of a variety of shapes, sizes and colors in every region of the island, and they were always fun to see, but that wasn't the main wildlife in my area. There were a variety of birds, geckos and lizards as well as a wide variety of moths and butterflies that you probably won't see anyone else in the world. I would also see the random flamingo from time to time and would frequently wake up in the middle of the night to the sound of hedgehogs munching on the hissing cockroaches that resided in my house.

Before Madagascar I had never seen a hissing cockroach (or a cockroach in general) so I was rather terrified of them until a couple months at my sight an American working for an NGO came by and told me what they were, then I felt foolish and relieved. The first couple weeks I tried to wage war on them but realized it was hopeless. After learning they were harmless I found them rather entertaining and didn't mind them so much. The rats were a different story though, every volunteer had their own stories and battles with the rats in their homes but we all learned how to deal. Most volunteers have an unspoken agreement with the rats of don't come out when I'm here and don't come onto my level while I'm here and working, you stay up in the rafter area and we'll be okay; however, if you venture down into my zone that is where I have the authority to kill you. The mouse/rat traps over there are seriously no joke!

I also was not prepared for the amount of fleas that I'd encounter nor was I prepared for the "parasy" or sand fleas that would plague everyone's feet and lay eggs under our skin. It sounds terrifying at first but I haven't heard of a single volunteer not having one at some point during their service. Besides, after your body learns what the itchy feeling of having one is like it's rather easy to get them off before they start to burrow. While I'm sure no one expected this to be the regular "wildlife" they would encounter while in Madagascar, I would say fleas, cockroaches and rats were probably the most common and sighted animals during service.

9

Getting Sick

Everyone gets sick at least once during their service and I won't lie, it sucks. A lot. And the Malagasy culture approaches sickness differently than we do in the States for if someone is sick everyone in the village will go visit them! It is the exact opposite of what we do in the States, and Malagasy think we are weird for not wanting to have visitors while we go through whatever sickness we have. As time went on I did come to understand and realize why the Malagasy will visit those that are ill and it is because not everybody survives from the flu or whatever sickness it is they have which is not typical in the States. In Madagascar, there is a larger danger of people actually dying from the illness or infection they have so people will go and be with those who are sick to not only try and boost their morale but to make sure they all say their goodbyes. I learned quickly to not let anyone know I was sick, as I honestly didn't want anyone coming over to keep me company, but I would go visit those I was close to anytime they were sick.

10

Reverse Culture Shock

Many people will try to prepare you for the immense shock you'll go through upon returning to the States, and you'll take a lot of it to heart and into consideration but nothing can truly prepare you for it. I think the culture shock was worse coming back to the States that it was going to Madagascar! Going from a place of scarcity, like in every sense of the word, back to a culture where convenience and abundance is everywhere, it is very jarring.

Many of us had panic attacks in the grocery stores seeing that much food and that many options all in one place; I learned I had to make very specific grocery lists with brand name and box size anytime I had to go shopping. People you don't know striking up conversation for no reason at all was suspicious, packing up all your stuff instead of asking someone nearby to keep an eye on it while you run to the bathroom was the norm, not remembering the English words you want to use in conversations and not being able to ignore questions you don't want to answer by playing dumb/like you don't understand what the person just said isn't an option anymore. Also getting used to reflective surfaces everywhere, clothing expectations and body image culture was difficult. Most returned volunteers have to take three to six months to readjust and figure out our next steps with life as well as the value of the dollar.

11

Realizing the Affect

I also wish I would have known beforehand how much this experience would affect the rest of my life. The experience I had in the Peace Corps shifted my entire perspective on life with gender roles, human rights, on food scarcity, what luxury is, and what in general is necessary to survive or to live in the world. In Madagascar one doesn't need a lot of clothes or possessions to be a part of something greater, they have communities and closeness and help one another even when they have no means to give. In my Malagasy village people truly lived a life of "what is mine is yours" and it's so different from what I was taught to believe in the States that I now walk with two different cultural perspectives.

My Peace Corps experience has also made me not care as much about "first world problems" such as a food order being wrong or having to wait for a delayed flight. While these things can be annoying from time to time, after experiencing third world problems, like not having any water to drink due to a drought or going to a three-year-old's funeral, I realized that there are completely different cultural and scales of problems. My service also made me aware of the socio-economic problems that I witnessed and experienced in Madagascar are also very real and present in the States; I was not prepared for that realization.

42

12

Conclusion

Everyone has their own story of discovery and reasoning for going into the Peace Corps; I'm sure Eleanor Bergstein, the writer and co-producer of Dirty Dancing, had no intent for the small reference she inserted at the beginning of the movie to have such a life changing effect on me but it did. While I was fortunate to have had the experience of a lifetime working in Madagascar I was very much not prepared for either the culture or the environment I wound up living three years of my life in. I hope this book is of some help to anyone either planning a trip to Madagascar or wanting to become a Peace Corps Volunteer have a better understanding of things to remember, what items to take with them and some expectations of what the experience may be like.

If you found this book helpful, I would be very appreciative if you left a favorable review for it on Amazon! If you would like to learn more about the Peace Corps, or read other personal accounts from volunteer's service, here are some other book recommendations:

· The Insiders Guide to the Peace Corps by Dillion Banerjee

- The Complete Guide to Joining the Peace Corps: What You Need to Know Explained Simply by Sharlee DiMenichi
- Nothing Works But Everything Works Out by Leigh Marie Dannhauser
- Slipping on the Ice: A Collection of Stories From a Peace Corps Ukraine Volunteer by Robert Minton
- A Five Finger Feast: Two Years in Kazakhstan, Lessons from the Peace Corps by Tim Suchsland
- It Depends: A Guide to Peace Corps by Kelly Branyik

Resources

1. Banerjee, D. (2009). *The Insider's Guide to the Peace Corps 2nd (second) edition Text Only* (Second Edition). Ten Speed Press.
2. DiMenichi, S. (2012). *The Complete Guide to Joining the Peace Corps: What You Need to Know Explained Simply* (Illustrated ed.). Atlantic Publishing Group, Inc.
3. BBC News. (2019, November 15). *Madagascar Country Profile.* Retrieved June 19, 2022, from https://www.bbc.com/news/world-africa-13861843
4. Butler, R. A. (2020). *Malagasy, the Language of Madagascar.* Wild-Madagascar.Org. Retrieved June 19, 2022, from https://www.wildmadagascar.org/people/malagasy.html
5. Covell, M. A. (2021, March 10). *Madagascar | History, Population, Languages, Map, & Facts.* Encyclopedia Britannica. Retrieved June 19, 2022, from https://www.britannica.com/place/Madagascar
6. Kramer, R. (2022). *Madagascar | Animals, People, and Threats | WWF.* World Wildlife Fund. Retrieved June 20, 2022, from https://www.worldwildlife.org/places/madagascar
7. *Madagascar.* (2022). Peace Corps. Retrieved June 20, 2022, from https://www.peacecorps.gov/madagascar/
8. *Madagascar - History.* (2021, March 10). Encyclopedia Britannica. Retrieved June 20, 2022, from https://www.britannica.com/place/Madagascar/History
9. Peace Corps. (2022, June 23). *9 questions about serving as an*

LGBTQIA+ Volunteer, answered. Retrieved June 24, 2022, from
https://www.peacecorps.gov/stories/9-questions-about-serving
-as-an-lgbtqia-volunteer-answered/

10. Peace Corps. (n.d.). *Fast Facts.* Retrieved June 23, 2022, from
https://www.peacecorps.gov/news/fast-facts/

About the Author

Tatum Moorer served as an agricultural volunteer from 2009 to 2013 in the Androy Region (known as the Deep South) of Madagascar. She currently works as a landscape and urban designer in the greater Denver Metro Area in Colorado, USA, where she focuses on doing community outreach for creating spaces that preserve natural resources and improve the quality of life for communities.